KidCaps' Presents
The American Revolution

A History Just for Kids

KidCaps is An Imprint of BookCaps™

www.bookcaps.com

KIDCAPS

Copyright © 2012 by Golgotha Press, Inc.

Cover Image © mangostock - Fotolia.com

All rights reserved. This book or any portion thereof may not be reproduced or used in any manner whatsoever without the express written permission of the publisher except for the use of brief quotations in a book review.

Printed in the United States of America

The American Revolution

Table of Contents

About KidCaps 4
Introduction 6
Chapter 1: What led up to the American Revolution? 10
Chapter 2: Why did the American Revolution happen? 22
Chapter 3: What happened during the American Revolution? 28
Chapter 4: What was it like to be a kid during the American Revolution? 36
Chapter 5: How did the American Revolution end? 39
Chapter 6: What happened after the American Revolution? 42
Conclusion 46

KIDCAPS

ABOUT KIDCAPS

KidCaps is an imprint of BookCaps™ that is just for kids! Each month BookCaps will be releasing several books in this exciting imprint. Visit are website or like us on Facebook to see more!

The American Revolution

A fierce battle between the British and the American Colonists during the Revolutionary War[1]

---

[1] Image source: http://thebornagainamerican.blogspot.com/2011/04/theres-reason-we-fought-revolutionary.html

KIDCAPS

INTRODUCTION

The war was raging all around him. Johnny was only twelve years old, so he wasn't allowed to pick up a gun or to be a soldier. However, he still had a very important job on the battlefield: he was the messenger for American Major General Gates. While he waited for the scouts to come back with their reports of British troop movements, Johnny could hear the musket balls whizzing above him, breaking branches in the trees. His father was out there in the battle lines, and through the smoke on the field, Johnny could just barely see him finish loading his musket, step to the right, take aim, and fire the weapon. The gun rocked as it fired and let out a cloud of smoke as the black powder exploded in the barrel, pushing the musket out at high speed. Johnny's father stepped back behind a tree to reload his musket-

The American Revolution

something that took even the best trained soldier about twenty seconds to do- before coming out to fire again.

Johnny looked behind him and could just make out the shapes of the army tents in the distance. He knew that his mother and sister would be safe so far away from the action. He started to wonder if they were afraid, but then he didn't have much time to think as another volley of musket balls went flying towards the soldiers all around him. Three fell on the ground, yelling in pain. Thankfully, Johnny's father wasn't one of them. His father took advantage of the fact that the British would be reloading their guns and stepped out from behind the tree and fired another shot. On the other side of the field, about 50 yards away, Johnny thought that he saw an officer fall down from his horse. *Good shot dad!*

A shout from over his right shoulder snapped Johnny away from the battle and sent him running to a scout who had just arrived back from his mission. He had a piece of paper in his hand and gave is to Johnny as he said: "Take this message to the Major General right away. He has to know that the British are moving towards our left flank! Run, boy, run!"

Johnny took the paper from the scout's hand and ran as fast as he could towards Major General Gates' position on the left side of the battle line. He handed the Major General the message, who read it immediately. The Major General looked up from the note at the boy and told him that he had done a good job. He then shouted orders to move the riflemen and the New York and New

Hampshire divisions to the left. They would be ready when the British came.

Johnny had just given Major General Horatio Gates the information that he would need to defend the Americans against the British attack during the Second Battle of Saratoga. It was October 7, 1777, and the Americans were about to win their first major battle against the British army. Within a few short hours, the British General John Burgoyne would have to surrender his army to Major General Horatio Gates. It would be a moment to celebrate and would be destined to become a turning point in the American Revolutionary War.

Were you surprised to learn that kids were allowed on the battlefields during the Revolutionary War? If so, there may be other facts about the American Revolution that will surprise you as well. In this handbook, we will be looking closer at this important time during the very beginning of American history. As we do so, try to imagine what it would have been like to be alive back then. Don't just read the names and think of them as people from a faraway time; think about them as people just like you. When they had problems, they had to decide how to solve them. Sometimes they were right; and sometimes they were wrong, but they always tried to do what was best for the country.

We are going to learn a little about why the Revolutionary War was fought, and what happened during it. For example, did you know that not everyone thought that it was a good idea to fight against the British? In fact, some Americans tried to stop the Patriots from meeting

The American Revolution

together and going to the battlefield. As we will see, it was a time when lots of Americans had to decide what they stood for and what they would do about it.

We are going to be looking at some interesting new words also. As you read, keep your eyes peeled for the special words in **bold** letters. They will tell you about some of the important ideas and decisions that made the Americans revolt against the British. Every time that you see a word in **bold**, try to think about what *you* would have done if you were alive back then. Would you have supported it, fought against it, or stayed neutral (not supporting one side or the other)?

The story of the American Revolution helps us to understand the things that are the most important to the American people, both in the past and in the present. We will learn about the things that they were willing to die for, the very same things that should matter to us today. Are you ready to learn some more? Then let's start with a very important question: what led up to the American Revolution?

CHAPTER 1: WHAT LED UP TO THE AMERICAN REVOLUTION?

As you can probably imagine, something as important as the American Revolution did not start overnight and was not about just one thing. In fact, the seeds of the Revolution had been planted a long time before and had been growing in the hearts of the American Colonists for a long time. In this section, we are going to have a look at some of the important events that led up to the American Revolution and how they affected the people involved. Let's start with one of the earliest events: the **French and Indian War** (also called the Seven Years' War).

The American Revolution

By the mid-1700s, there were thirteen colonies in the New World and the Colonists were growing in number. They provided crops and other goods for England and were allowed to have a certain amount of self-governance (which meant that local governments that were allowed to make small day-to-day decisions). Although they lived very far away from London (the capital of the British Empire) the Colonists were still considered British citizens. When a fight broke out between British colonists and French colonists in the New World, both countries refused to back down. Native Americans (called "Indians" back then) sided with the French, while the American Colonists stayed loyal to the British.

The War finally ended in 1763. It had cost a lot of money for everyone involved, but the British did not expect the Colonists to help them pay for that. What the British did expect, however, was that the Colonists help with paying for British soldiers to stay in the area to protect them from any further violence. As part of actions to end the War and to make sure that there wouldn't be any more fighting, King George III issued the "**Royal Proclamation of 1763**" on October 7, 1763. Among other things, it told the Colonists that, in order to keep peace with the Native Americans that they had been fighting with, that they couldn't go any further West than the Appalachian Mountains (which formed part of the Western border of many of the thirteen colonies).

In order to get the tax money used to pay for soldiers, the British passed the **Stamp Act of 1765**, which required the Colonists to use special "stamped" paper for official documents, newspapers, and magazines. The Colonists had to buy this paper only from the British and only with British money.

Also, the British passed a series of laws called the **Townshend Acts** during 1767 and 1768 in order to get more money from the Colonists. Included in these acts were laws allowing British representatives to board American boats and to enter American homes and businesses to look for contraband (illegal stuff). They would look for tea, sugar, and molasses that were being sold without British permission (which meant "without first paying British taxes". Americans started to resent (to feel angry about) the constant invasions of their privacy and about always being treated like they were the enemy.

So far, we have seen that the French and Indian War had two major consequences for American colonists:
- They had to pay for British soldiers to stay in the area to protect them
- They couldn't move any further west than they already had

As we will see, both of those consequences made the colonists very upset with their British rulers.

The Townshend Acts that we saw above, which were designed to make sure that the colonies stayed under British rule and did exactly as they were told, made the Colonists living in Boston especially upset. Boston was a shipping town, so it had to deal with all of the restrictions that came from the Townshend Acts. They had

The American Revolution

to pay high tariffs (fees) for stuff made in Britain and they had to deal with British representatives always boarding their ships and entering their shops, treating them like common criminals. The local government in Massachusetts began to pass around a letter asking the other colonies to join with them in resisting these new acts.

The British started to feel like the colonies were getting out of control and that stronger action was needed. They seized a boat used for shipping goods and said that its owner (future Patriot John Hancock) was guilty of smuggling goods and of not paying the proper taxes to the British government. The people in Boston couldn't take it anymore and they began to riot in the streets. A large British warship in Boston Harbor had already been forcing American sailors to go work on it, but now the colonists felt that seizing John Hancock's ship was the last straw. They scared the British representatives so much that the representatives ran away and hid in a safe place until British soldiers came later and rescued them.

To respond to the riots, the British government sent a large number of troops to the city to maintain law and order and to make sure that everyone knew that they were still in charge. Things were very tense, and you can imagine how the Colonists felt every time that they saw the soldiers marching up and down the streets of Boston in their bright red coats. The Colonists felt like prisoners in their own houses, like they couldn't even live their lives and do what they wanted. Would you like to have lived like that?

One day, on March 5, 1770, something very important happened: British soldiers fired on a crowd of Colonists during a protest in Boston. Six colonists died and five more were injured before the violence ended. Called **"The Boston Massacre"**, the event made a lot of people think that the British troops, instead of protecting the Colonists as they were being paid to do, were acting more like slave owners. The Colonists, not only in Boston but in in other colonies as well, felt that the British government only cared about money and power, and not about the welfare (the happiness and prosperity) of the American people.

In June of 1772, one of the British ships that had been in charge of enforcing the unpopular regulations and laws got into a little bit of a problem. It ran aground in Rhode Island and got stuck. The locals attacked the ship to show their frustration with the way that they were being treated. They made the crew get off the boat, they stole everything of value, and then they burned the ship to the ground.

The destruction of the ship, called the **HMS Gaspée**, marked a turning point in the way that the British dealt with American rebellion. Instead of simply enduring the bad behavior or just passing a law, the British decided that an example should be made. It was determined that those responsible for burning the HMS Gaspée were going to be taken to England and tried as traitors to their country. Although the British ended up not having enough evidence to go to trial, the Colonists were horrified that the British would even think of taking American Colonists all the way to England to have British

The American Revolution

judges decide what should happen to them for things they did while thousands of miles away in America.

In November of 1772, Samuel Adams and Dr. Joseph Warren, seeing that the British government was threatening to invalidate the local government and judges who were operating in the colonies, formed the Massachusetts **"Committee of Correspondence"**. Other colonies soon did the same. These Committees allowed the colonies to talk to each other and share ideas without any British loyalists (called "Tories") being able to spy on them and report back to their superiors. By 1773, it was clear that these secretive Committees had become more important than the official governments. They were used later to organize the meeting of the First Continental Congress and to plan out what action should be taken.

In 1773, another law passed in Britain made its way to the colonies- and again, it was a law that made people very angry. The law was called **"The Tea Act"** and was approved by the King on May 10, 1773. The Tea Act was an extension of the Townshend Acts. As we saw above, the Townshend Acts raised taxes and limited the movement of certain goods, including tea. However, the Tea Act made sure that Colonists would only be able to buy tea directly from the East India Company, who had a special agreement with the British government. What's more, the colonists would have to pay a certain tax to buy the tea.

Although the price was actually pretty good, the colonists didn't like the *precedent* that would be set if they accepted the tea offered under the Tea Act. What does that mean? A *precedent* is like an example that will be followed. The Colonists were worried that if they paid the tea tax that the British imposed on the Americans (without first asking) then it would be like saying: "Go ahead and do whatever you like to us without first asking what we think about it."

When the first shipments of the newly taxed tea arrived in American ports, everyone refused to accept it. They either sent it back or took it and put it into a warehouse, either way refusing to pay the taxes. In Boston, however, the Colonists took even stronger action: they threw the tea into the harbor. Do you know what that special night in Boston was called? It was called the "**Boston Tea Party.**" What happened during this very special "party"? On the night of December 16, 1773, about 130 men, dressed as Native Americans (to show that they were loyal to the New World and not to England) dumped 342 chests of tea into the salty water of Boston Harbor. The tea was valued at about $1.4 million, and it shocked the British to see such disrespect to the Crown and to see the destruction of so much valuable tea.

The American Revolution

The destruction of 342 chests of tea on December 16, 1773[2]

In order to bring the increasingly rebellious colonies back under control, English Parliament (with the permission of the King) passed a series of laws called **The Intolerable Acts**. These laws restricted the freedoms of the Colonists, especially those in Boston, more than ever. Two of them in particular, **The Boston Port Act** and **The Quartering Act**, fanned the flames of revolution that were beginning to burn hotter and hotter. What did these two acts mean for people living in Boston?

The Boston Port Act closed Boston harbor until the East India Company was paid back for the tea that had been destroyed during the Boston Tea Party. Although it was fair that the East India Company be reimbursed for the tea, do you think it was fair to punish the *entire city of Boston* for the actions of about 130 men? Do you think

---

[2] Image source: http://en.wikipedia.org/wiki/Boston_Tea_Party#Destruction_of_the_tea

that the Colonists living in Boston should at least have had the opportunity to explain *why* they did what they did? The Boston Port Act punished everyone and there was nothing the Colonists could do to stop it.

The Quartering Act required that British soldiers be housed in any unoccupied building in any of the thirteen colonies. Thus, the Colonists were forced have soldiers as their neighbors. Also, the British soldiers would also "requisition" anything that they wanted from the locals. Although they would pay the locals a price that was determined to be a "fair rate", the colonists still felt that they were being forced to pay for something that they didn't want in the first place- protection provided by British soldiers.

As all of the colonies began to suffer the effects of the Intolerable Acts, the Committees of Correspondence called a special meeting. They wanted to have representatives of all thirteen colonies get together and talk about how to respond to the increasingly harsh demands from the British. This meeting was called **The First Continental Congress** and was held on September 5, 1774 in Philadelphia, Pennsylvania. 56 members (representing all of the colonies but Georgia) attended and showed their support.

The Colonists still wanted to remain loyal to England, so there was no talk of rebellion at this meeting. However, they knew that things couldn't go on as they had been. They decided to ask the King for help, and that they would meet again the next year if things hadn't gotten better. This first Congress was important because it al-

The American Revolution

lowed the Colonists to organize themselves and to feel united. Although each colony had its own needs and problems, they all agreed that England was going too far and was asking too much from the colonies.

Although they had planned to have a second congress during the next year to discuss what they would do if England didn't change, events unfolded quickly during the next few months. Tensions that had been building up in Boston exploded into the first official battle of the Revolutionary War. How did it happen?

In the early months of the year following the First Constitutional Convention (1775) British soldiers in Boston were getting more and more worried about the colonists and about what they might do. The soldiers began to have regular military drills and to move more and more troops to the city. The Colonists, for their part, began to train larger "militias", which were like armies made up of local residents. The militias began to practice and drill also.

On April 14, 1775, the British soldiers received instructions to march to the nearby town of Concord in order to confiscate a large supply of weapons that the colonists were thought to have had there, and also to arrest some of the "leaders" of the rebellion (including Samuel Adams and John Hancock). On the night of April 18, around 700 troops began the journey to the towns of Lexington and Concord. The Lexington and Concord militias (having been warned about the troops by brave colonists like Paul Revere) had already moved the weapons to another town and were ready for the soldiers when they came.

A tense standoff ended in a fight when the British troops marched through Lexington, leaving eight colonists dead and ten more wounded, while only one British soldier was wounded in the fight. When the British arrived at Concord, however, things were different. This time, militias from other towns joined the Concord militia as the British searched for the weapons they had come for. The British soldiers, as they saw the militia getting bigger and bigger, started to fire on them. The militia, surprised that the soldiers were shooting to kill, fired back. By the time the British soldiers retreated back to Boston, 73 soldiers were dead and another 174 had been wounded. Although 49 colonists had been killed and 39 wounded, it was a definite American victory. Soon, militia from all over New England went to Boston and completely surrounded the city. **The Battle of Lexington and Concord** marked the moment when the rebellion changed from talk to real action.

The American Revolution

Americans firing on British soldiers during the Battle of Lexington and Concord[3]

The next month, during the **Second Continental Congress** that began meeting on May 10, 1775, it was decided that the battle that began in Lexington and Concord had to continue. An army was organized, a general (George Washington) was chosen, and a final offer of peace was sent to the King of Britain. Finally, after all other efforts to avoid more fighting ended, a **Declaration of Independence** from Britain was approved by all thirteen colonies on July 4, 1776.

The American Revolution had officially begun.

---

[3] Image source: http://www.shsu.edu/~his_ncp/LexCon.html

CHAPTER 2: WHY DID THE AMERICAN REVOLUTION HAPPEN?

Although we have seen some of the *events* that led up to the American Revolution, we haven't really looked too much at the *reasons* for it. In this section, we will look at the "why" of the American Revolution. In other words, why were so many people willing to fight and die for American independence? Let's find out.

The American Revolution didn't start out with a war; that's where it ended. The American Revolution started with an *idea*: that all people have natural rights. The founding fathers and colonists were really influenced by

The American Revolution

the writings of a man named John Locke. He wrote a very influential and important book in 1689 called *Two Treatises of Government*. His book made some important points that got a lot of colonists excited and thinking about trying to change the way things were being done in the New World. Two of the ideas that Locke mentioned in his book were that:

- All men are created equal
- A legitimate government can only exist when it has the consent of the people

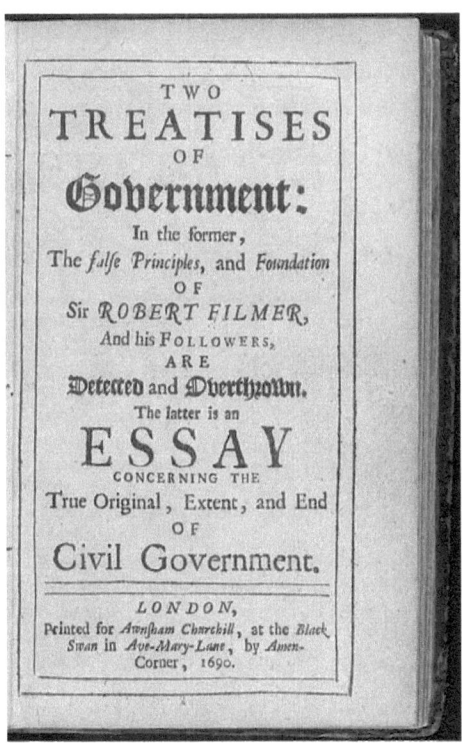

The book written by John Locke in 1689 was called *Two Treatises of Government*[4]

These points went directly against everything that the British government was doing to the American colonists. By making the American colonists accept a King that it didn't want and by treating them as inferior, the colonists felt that the rule of Britain was no longer legitimate; in other words, it could be overthrown! Without the consent (permission) of the people, British laws meant nothing.

The idea that the governed should have a say in how the government operated was actually started by the British themselves. When they sent the original colonists to Jamestown in 1607, they allowed the colonists to form a local government that would let them decide how to run things in the New World. When Parliament and the King later tried to take away the very freedoms that the Colonists had grown used to, it was forcing a man to learn how to crawl like a baby again. It was not fair and it upset everybody in the New World. It certainly did not treat them like equals. At best, it treated them like servants, or even like slaves.

The biggest problem, as the Colonists saw it, was that they had no representation in British Parliament. Remember that at first, the colonies never even thought of independence; they just wanted to have a say in the decisions that would be affecting them and their families. When the Stamp Tax was passed in 1765, no one both-

---

[4] Image source:
http://en.wikipedia.org/wiki/Two_Treatises_of_Government

The American Revolution

ered to ask the Colonists if they wanted to pay more taxes so that soldiers could protect them. When the Tea Act was passed in 1773, no one asked the Colonists if they liked buying tea from the East India Company and if they were okay paying the extra tax.

No one asked the Colonists if they liked the King, or who they thought should be in charge of Parliament. No one asked their opinion about the wars in Europe or about where British soldiers should sleep at night and where they should get their food. Britain felt that the Colonists had "virtual representation" because British politicians "always" acted in favor of their citizens. However, the many harsh laws passed against the Americans showed that this was not the case at all. Rather, British politicians seemed to be concerned only with getting more money and with making sure that everyone knew that they were the ones in charge.

In America, there was also a fear that the British politicians would become corrupt if given too much power and that the citizens needed to be there to make sure that things didn't get out of hand. However, when they weren't allowed even to vote, how could the colonists fight corruption? The last straw came when England threatened to take Colonists away to Britain to face punishment after the burning of the HMS Gaspée. It was like Britain was saying: "I will decide when and how I listen to you."

What do you think? Did the American Colonists have a right to feel upset about the things that were happening to them? Should the British have treated the Colonists with more respect and given them an opportunity to talk about how the government was being run?

As time went by, the Colonists decided that they would try to form their own government that would respect the "natural rights" of all its citizens. In the Declaration of Independence, look at some of the reasons that the Founding Fathers used to explain why they thought independence from Britain was necessary. See if you can see some of the ideas of John Locke either directly mentioned or at least hinted at:

> We hold these truths to be self-evident, that <u>all men are created equal, that they are endowed by their Creator with certain unalienable Rights</u>, that among these are Life, Liberty and the pursuit of Happiness.--That to secure these rights, Governments are instituted among Men, <u>deriving their just powers from the consent of the governed</u>, --That whenever any Form of Government becomes destructive of these ends, it is the Right of the People to alter or to abolish it, and to institute new Government, laying its foundation on such principles and organizing its powers in such form, as to them shall seem most likely to effect their Safety and Happiness."[5]

The American Revolution wasn't just about taxes or tea; it was about the very *idea* that all people deserved something better than what the British government was giv-

---

[5] Declaration of Independence text: http://www.archives.gov/exhibits/charters/declaration_transcript.html

The American Revolution

ing them. The Colonists felt that they deserved to have a voice in the way that they lived their lives and in the way that they were treated. When no one gave them this and when no one listened to them, they did the only thing they could do: they declared their independence and formed a new nation.

CHAPTER 3: WHAT HAPPENED DURING THE AMERICAN REVOLUTION?

The American Revolution was about ideas, but it was fought with weapons. Strong and brave men on both sides of the war used muskets, cannons, and military tactics to try to make sure that their ideas were listened to. The British fought to keep the rebellious American colonies under their control, and the Americans fought to get the freedom that they were sure that they deserved.

Although there were many battles during the Revolutionary War, a few of them were more important than

The American Revolution

the others. For example, do you remember what happened after the Battle of Lexington and Concord? After the fighting had ended, the British troops retreated back to Boston and the Colonist militias (numbering almost 15,000 soldiers) surrounded the city and wouldn't let any British soldiers leave it. By the next month (May 1775) there were about 6,000 British troops occupying the city of Boston.

While the British worked on plans to break out of the city, the Colonists worked on how to get into it. On the night of June 16, they decided to sneak a group of soldiers up onto to a hill in the nearby town of Charleston, where a Colonist spy had said the British would try to escape. Sure enough, on the afternoon of June 17, 1775, the British saw that the Colonists were trying to block their escape and decided to attack.

The Colonist militia had dug trenches on Breed's Hill, knowing that it would allow them to defend their position and maybe even to fire cannons down into the occupied city of Boston. When the British sailed from Boston to Charleston and landed their little boats on the peninsula near the hill, everyone knew that there was going to be a fight. More militia came, but it was not easy to understand where everyone was supposed to go. Some got stuck crossing a bridge when the British began to fire on it; others stayed at the nearby Bunker Hill; and still others came to the fight but then didn't obey the orders of the officers in charge.

Because they had limited ammunition, the Colonists had received this order: "Don't fire until you see the whites of their eyes". Because the muskets weren't as accurate when firing over long distances, the militia was supposed to wait until the soldiers were very close before firing their weapons. Would you have been afraid to see the enemy so close and not be able to do anything about it?

The first two attempts by the British were devastating to their ranks, with some groups losing 75-90% of their soldiers. However, during their third attempt, the Colonists started to run out of ammunition. One of the Colonist officers even got into a swordfight with a British soldier got very close to him and then tried to stab him with a bayonet. The Colonists retreated back towards Bunker Hill, leaving their cannons and tools behind. It was at this point when a lot of the militia men were killed.

By 5PM, only two hours after it had begun, the fighting had ended. Although the British had won the position, they had done so at a very high price: 226 soldiers (including 19 officers) had been killed, and another 828 had been wounded. In other words, about 1,000 men (or 1/6 of the fighting force stationed in Boston) couldn't fight in the War anymore.

For their part, the Colonists had lost 115 men, and another 305 had been wounded. However, this battle (called **The Battle of Bunker Hill**) surprised everyone in Britain and showed that the Colonists were to be taken seriously. It made them realize that this war would not be over in just a few days.

The American Revolution

The Colonist militias defending their position on Breed's Hill[6]

Another important battle was the one we mentioned in the introduction: **The Second Battle of Saratoga** which was fought on October 7, 1777. During this battle, the Colonists had a major victory, leading to the surrender of a British General and his 6,000 troops. This battle was a major turning point in the Revolutionary War because it showed that the Colonists had a very good chance of winning. As a direct result of this war, the French decided to declare war on Britain and to help the Americans. Why was this so important?

Well, by this time (over one year after the fighting had begun) the Continental Army (the American soldiers) was starting to have real money problems. They needed more weapons and ammunition, as well as uniforms. Plus, the British soldiers just kept on coming, and there was little that the Americans could do to stop it. Why couldn't they stop more British soldiers from coming?

---

[6] Image source: http://www.glogster.com/luismcneil/battle-of-bunker-hill/g-6mcq8mj5ukota1c15h9e3a0?old_view=True

While the Americans were fighting very well on land, there was practically nothing that they could do on the water. The British ships kept bringing more soldiers and more supplies and the Americans couldn't stop them. But when the French joined the Americans in fighting the British, they brought with them fresh troops, weapons, clothing, and lots of ships to protect the coast and to fight off the enemy.

The French especially helped during **The Siege of Yorktown** which lasted from September 28 – October 19, 1781. During this time, French ships defeated a British fleet, cutting off any escape or reinforcements for the soldiers stationed there. Then, a combined force of over 15,000 French and American soldiers surrounded the city of Yorktown, until the General there, Lieutenant General Lord Cornwallis, was forced to surrender. He and his more than 7,000 troops were captured, and the major fighting in the New World ended.

During the Revolutionary War, the soldiers who fought got to show who they really were. Instead of just pretending to be nice people, or brave, or loyal, they got to demonstrate in very tough times what kind of person they were on the *inside*. For example, let's look at **General George Washington** (who later became the first President of the United States).

The American Revolution

A portrait of George Washington, the man who commanded the troops during the Revolutionary War[7]

George Washington was born in Virginia, and served in the military during the French and Indian War. He had the reputation of being a man who was loyal to his country and not to himself. During the War, he sacrificed a lot and proved what kind of man he really was. For example, towards the end of the War, some of his soldiers felt that the newly established government wasn't caring very well for them. Knowing that Washington was a good man who loved his men, a secret letter

---

[7] Image Source: http://en.wikipedia.org/wiki/George_Washington

was written and given to him on May 22, 1782. The letter stated that some of Washington's men thought that he should become the next King of the United States. Did Washington accept the offer?

George Washington showed what type of man he truly was by rejecting the offer and encouraging his men to be loyal to the government they had fought to establish. Thus, Washington set a great example for all future leaders of the United States: every one of them should think about what's good for the country before he thinks about what's good for himself.

However, another man did just the opposite during the American Revolution; his name was **Benedict Arnold**. Benedict Arnold was a brave General who fought with the Continental Army in many important battles, including the Battles of Saratoga. He used his own money during the War, and was even injured in the leg. As he recovered in Philadelphia, Arnold began to complain about the way that he had been treated and about how the new country was turning out. He thought that the United States was going to be defeated by the British before much more time had passed. In the meantime, General Washington put him in charge of the important military fort of West Point.

On September 23, 1780, a British officer was captured with secret papers that had been given to him. The papers showed him exactly how to attack the fort at West Point and promised him safe passage anywhere he wanted go. How did the enemy get such detailed infor-

The American Revolution

mation about the fort? The papers had come from Benedict Arnold.

Within a short time, Benedict Arnold escaped punishment and went to the other side of the war, fighting with the British. He later met his fellow Americans on the battlefield and even destroyed parts of Virginia in the terrible fighting that followed. Can you imagine how sad his fellow soldiers must have felt to see their former friend leading enemy troops against them and firing his own gun at them? Truly, Benedict Arnold showed who he was on the inside: someone who only thinks about himself, and not others.

The Revolutionary War was about ideas, but it was fought with very real guns, soldiers, and cannons.

CHAPTER 4: WHAT WAS IT LIKE TO BE A KID DURING THE AMERICAN REVOLUTION?

Do you remember twelve year-old Johnny from the introduction? Although Johnny was not a real person, there were lots of boys and girls just like him who helped the United States to win their independence from Great Britain.

The American Revolution

Young boys often played the drum as American soldiers marched from one place to another[8]

Have you ever wondered what it would have been like to have lived back then? Then let's take a few minutes and see what it was like to be a kid during the American Revolution.

Because the War was being fought everywhere, sometimes it wasn't safe for families to stay at home while the father went off to war. As a result, it wasn't strange to see an entire family travelling with a father who was a soldier. But what would the family actually do while travelling with the army? What could the kids do to help the soldiers win independence and freedom for everybody? Let's find out.

While travelling with the army, the mothers and daughters focused on very important jobs like preparing healthy meals, fixing torn clothes, and washing the tents and laundry (sometimes for the entire army). They made sure that the soldiers would be ready to fight the next day and that they could rest well each night.

---

[8] Image source:
http://www.carolinaconnoisseur.com/revolutionary-war.htm

What about the boys? As we saw earlier, boys would often play music while marching and would work as messengers during the actual fighting. However, during times of peace, the boys would get firewood, carry buckets of water, and help to pack everything up when it was time to move and to take it apart when they were done.

Would you have been scared to march with the army, knowing that another attack could come at any time? Would you have run away, or would you have done your part to help the United States to win? Like we learned with George Washington and Benedict Arnold, the Revolutionary War gave everyone- even boys and girls- the chance to show who they really were on the inside. If you had stayed to help the fight even though you were scared, you would have been just like General George Washington.

Even though they never picked up a gun or marched onto the battlefield, kids during the American Revolution did a lot of important things to help the men who were fighting to win the war.

The American Revolution

CHAPTER 5: HOW DID THE AMERICAN REVOLUTION END?

As we saw, the fighting in the United States ended on October 19, 1781 when Lieutenant General Lord Cornwallis surrendered and his troops were taken prisoner in Yorktown, Virginia. The French helped the United States to win a strong victory. However, the fighting continued in other parts of the world between France and Britain. In the meantime, there were still lots of British soldiers in the United States, kind of just hanging out. It was really weird, because no one knew if the fighting was going to start up again at any minute. George Washington was too afraid to send his troops home in case the British decided to attack again, but he knew that his men desperately wanted to see their families.

Finally, in 1783, representatives from the United States and Britain decided to get together in Paris to sign a treaty and to officially bring an end to the Revolutionary War. Called **The Treaty of Paris**, this document was signed on September 3, 1783. It had ten important points[9] that can be summed up as follows[10]:

1. Acknowledging the United States to be free, sovereign and independent states, and that the British Crown and all heirs and successors relinquish claims to the Government, propriety, and territorial rights of the same, and every part thereof;
2. Establishing the boundaries between the United States and British North America;
3. Granting fishing rights to United States fishermen in the Grand Banks, off the coast of Newfoundland and in the Gulf of Saint Lawrence;
4. Recognizing the lawful contracted debts to be paid to creditors on either side;
5. The Congress of the Confederation will "earnestly recommend" to state legislatures to recognize the rightful owners of all confiscated lands "provide for the restitution of all estates, rights, and

---

[9] Full document text source:
http://www.ourdocuments.gov/doc.php?doc=6&page=transcript
[10] Document summation source:
http://en.wikipedia.org/wiki/Treaty_of_Paris_(1783)

The American Revolution

   properties, which have been confiscated belonging to real British subjects [Loyalists]";
6. United States will prevent future confiscations of the property of Loyalists;
7. Prisoners of war on both sides are to be released and all property left by the British army in the United States unmolested (including slaves);
8. Great Britain and the United States were each to be given perpetual access to the Mississippi River;
9. Territories captured by Americans subsequent to treaty will be returned without compensation;
10. Ratification of the treaty was to occur within six months from the signing by the contracting parties.

Obviously, the most important of these points was the first one: the United States would be recognized from that moment on as an independent nation, and the British government needed to respect it as such. Wow! What an important document. All of the fighting, all of the secret meetings, committees of correspondence, and sacrifice had led them to this moment: the United States was free!

After the treaty was signed, the British soldiers left, and the Americans were alone in their new country. They immediately set to work building a better government.

CHAPTER 6: WHAT HAPPENED AFTER THE AMERICAN REVOLUTION?

After the American Revolution, one of the first major jobs that had to be taken care of was creating a new **constitution** for the country. Do you know what a constitution is a set of laws that decide how the government will be organized, as well as what the government can and cannot do. On September 17, 1787, a group of representatives from twelve of the thirteen colonies (Rhode Island stayed home) approved a new document for all of the state legislatures to approve.

The American Revolution

The signing of the U.S. Constitution. Do you see George Washington on the stage?[11]

This new Constitution was a very special document, as it provided for a way of life completely different from what the Americans had known under Great Britain. Do you remember some of the reasons why the Revolutionary War was fought? As we learned, it was because the people had no representation in
their government and because they were forced to accept decisions and laws that they did not like. The new Constitution made sure that those two problems would never happen again.

First, the Constitution created two separate places where representatives of each state could get together and talk about new laws and decisions. One, called the **House of Representatives**, would be based on the population of each state. The second, called the **Senate**, was a place

---

[11] Image source:
http://en.wikipedia.org/wiki/United_States_Constitution

where all the states had equal representation, no matter what their size was.

The American people felt good because now they would have a voice in their government. Instead of being forced to pay for things (like protection from British soldiers) that they didn't want, and being forced to do things (like giving the soldiers housing, food, and buying tea from only one company) the Americans themselves could decide what laws they would follow and which ones were unfair.

The Constitution also fixed the other problem: having a government that they were not happy with. The American people, under their new government, could change their leader if they weren't happy with them (something that they could never had done with the King of England). They could get rid of old laws or even whole sections of the Constitution if they no longer applied, and they could decide for themselves who they would trade with and buy from.

When the states approved the Constitution it was a real time to celebrate. It was like seeing all of their dreams come true. Although the new country wasn't perfect, it was a first step towards building something the world had never seen, a great experiment in republicanism (representation of the people in government). The United States would be like a bright light that other nations could look at and model their own government after.

What do you think: has the great experiment been a success? Thanks to the freedoms enjoyed since the Ameri-

The American Revolution

can Revolution, the United States has seen strong businesses growing, exciting new technologies being invented, and all sorts of opinions being expressed. Although you may not like or agree with everything that your fellow Americans do or say, you can always respect their right to say and do those things. After all, you can do and say what *you* want because of those same freedoms.

After the Revolutionary War ended, one of the most important things for the next generation to do was to remember how much the soldiers and politicians back then had sacrificed for us today. As the soldiers dies, people began to write books about the things that they had done and to give them large statutes and memorials. They named cities and even entire states after some of those men, and tried hard to never ever forget them.

July 4 (the anniversary of the day when the Declaration of Independence was adopted) became a national holiday, and people today still celebrate what the War accomplished. They think about what makes the United States so special, and they try to always appreciate the freedoms that other people don't have.

After the American Revolution, each generation has tried hard to be like George Washington, Thomas Jefferson, Benjamin Franklin, and Patrick Henry. They try hard to think about what is good for the country as a whole, and not just their own personal preferences. As a result, the "great experiment" of the United States continues to be an amazing success!

CONCLUSION

After having learned so much about the American Revolution, what do you think: was it the right thing to do to declare independence from Great Britain and to fight that long and difficult War? A lot of people living back then actually wanted to stay with the British because it was easier than fighting. However, other people (like the founding fathers) tried to look further into the future and try to see how the decision that they made could affect their children, grandchildren, and beyond. They realized the same thing that we have to realize: what we do today will affect tomorrow.

Of course, none of us are living under the same difficult situation that those Colonists were dealing with. However, we still have to make some tough decisions from

The American Revolution

time to time, and we have to be brave. Sometimes, the right thing to do isn't always easy; sometimes it's easier to run away (like Benedict Arnold did). But a great lesson that we learned from this handbook is how to stand up for what you believe in.

Today, Americans can vote in both state and national elections. They can choose who will be their leaders and what the new laws should be. Have you ever asked your mom or dad about voting, and how they decide who to vote for? Some parents choose not to vote, and that's okay too. After all, the point of living in the United States is that the government will not try to make people do anything that they don't want to.

In this handbook, we have learned how the American people fought back against the tyrants who wanted to take advantage of them and to mistreat them. We saw how even kids could help to change history, and how no matter how hard it is, we should always fight for what we believe in.

Will you be like George Washington and do the same?

George Washington leading his men during the Revolutionary War[12]

---

[12] Image source: http://www.sonofthesouth.net/revolutionary-war/battles/valley-forge.htm

www.ingramcontent.com/pod-product-compliance
Lightning Source LLC
Chambersburg PA
CBHW060507080526
44584CB00015B/1589